CAN ANIMALS AND MACHINES BE PERSONS?

CAN ANIMALS
AND MACHINES
BE PERSONS?

A Dialogue by

JUSTIN LEIBER

HACKETT PUBLISHING COMPANY

1985

Copyright © 1985 by Justin Leiber
All Rights Reserved

Designed by Mark E. Van Halsema
Cover design by Jackie Lacy
Typeset by Publishers Service, Bozeman, Montana
Printed in the United States of America
For further information please address
Hackett Publishing Company, Inc.
P. O. Box 44937
Indianapolis, Indiana 46204

Library of Congress Cataloging-in-Publication Data

Leiber, Justin.
    Can animals and machines be persons?

    Bibliography: p.
    1. Persons. 2. Animals, Treatment of—Philosophy.
3. Cybernetics—Moral and ethical aspects. I. Title.
BD331.L44   1985   126   85-21888
ISBN 0-87220-003-5
ISBN 0-87220-002-7 (pbk.)

To My Daughter,
Arlynn Melody Patrick
on Her Graduation from
Northwestern University Law School
and Her Accession to the Bar of the
State of Illinois.

Like Diamonds,
We Are Cut by Our Own Dust.

CONTENTS

Introduction

This is a dialogue about the notion of a person, of an entity that thinks and feels and acts, that counts and is accountable. Equivalently, it is about the *intentional idiom* —the well-knit fabric of terms that we use to characterise persons. Human beings are usually persons (a brain-dead human might be considered a human but not a person). But there may be persons, in various senses, that are not human beings. Much recent discussion has focused on hypothetical computer-robots and on the actual nonhuman great apes. The tenor of the discussion is naturalistic in that count, and accountability are, at least initially, presumed to be naturally well-knit with the possession of a cognitive and affective life. Otherwise, my aim has been to introduce some of the ideas that have sparked recent discussions.

For a critical reading and/or helpful comments, I thank Noam Chomsky, Daniel Dennett, and Marvin Minsky; my colleagues, James W. Garson, William Nelson, and M. G. Yoes, Jr.; and my one-time students, Mary Lloyd and Derrellyn Yates.

I am grateful, too, for a Faculty Development Leave from the University of Houston which supported composition of this work.

The Setting

This is the transcript of a hearing before the United Nations Space Administration Commission, established in the last decade of the twentieth century to consider claims arising in space and hence beyond the legal scope of any particular terrestrial nation. The concern of this hearing is the "rights of persons" on the UNSA's permanent satellite space community, Finland Station. This hearing takes place at the international launch station a few miles south of Quito, Ecuador—a launch site whose position on the earth's equator, at an elevation of nearly 10,000 feet, offers what ballistic scientists call a "slingshot" effect, with a significant saving in the enormous cost of raising mass into orbit over the northern hemisphere launch sites of the great powers. The Commissioners are Wai Chin, Barbara Hershell, Juan Mendez, Indira Ramajan, and Klaus Versen. The complainants are represented by Counselor Mary Godwin of Amnesty International and the International Civil Liberties Union. The respondent, represented by Counselor Peter Goodman, is Humanico, a corporation formed by UNSA to administer the Finland Station.

THE FIRST MORNING

COMMISSIONER KLAUS VERSEN: Counselors, I want to remind you both of two matters. First, this commission is not bound by the statutes or legal precedents of particular nations. In the present case, we can do nothing but make the best of the generality "respect for the basic rights of persons" (UNSA Statute 135.4). Second—a paradox that follows from the first point—we are more interested in philosophical than specifically legal argument. Indeed, our understanding is that there is no dispute about the more literal facts of the case. Perhaps I should run through those facts right now.

As you'll recall, shortly after Finland Station's assemblage in earth orbit, Humanico Corporation rocketed up the young female chimpanzee, Washoe-Delta, to research the long-term effects of weightlessness and to determine if her body might serve in the manufacture of organic chemicals. At that same time the Turing 346 computing system of Finland Station set into operation. Turing 346, a seventh-generation computer with video-sensor inputs and motorized outputs, soon came to seem another, and valued, member of the crew to the humans aboard Finland Station. They called it "AL." Among its many duties, AL was designed to befriend other crew members, to learn how to understand their problems and help them, while assisting more official projects as well. Perhaps inevitably, the human crew members came to think of AL as a person and friend.

More as a matter of natural than human design, Washoe-Delta also came to endear herself to the human

crew. Several taught her a portion of American sign language, supplemented with spacesuit hand signals. Humanico supported this informal experiment as a way of maintaining Washoe-Delta's health and docility—and, hence, her utility in hormone production.

After several months in weightlessness the cardiovascular system suffers irreversible changes. Consequently, the human crew of Finland Station have been returned to earth at regular intervals. But, because of the considerable cost, Humanico decided not to do this with Washoe-Delta. She has been in Finland Station for several years. Now she can only live in weightlessness. Washoe-Delta's situation is that of AL, the Station's Turing 346 system, for AL was assembled of necessity in space and cannot function in earth gravity. For reasons of economy and efficiency, Humanico Corporation now plans to shut down Finland Station.

Unexpectedly, at least for Humanico, some human crew members protested to Amnesty International and the International Civil Liberties Union. Counselor Mary Godwin comes before us with the complaint that Humanico must not terminate the operation of Finland Station, because (1) Washoe-Delta and AL "think and feel" and as such (2) "are persons," and hence (3) "their termination would violate their 'rights as persons.' " The commission feels free to entertain argument without as yet deciding whether, as Counselor Goodman has suggested, "the complaint is frivolous on its face."

Counselors, I again want to remind you that this is not a courtroom. My notes tell me you both graduated from Harvard Law School, Goodman in 1988 and Godwin seven years later. I hope you spent some time in Emerson Hall, where the philosophers hold forth.

I see three questions. One, do either Washoe-Delta or AL "think" or "feel"? Two, in virtue of their cognitive and emotional life, is either a person? Third, if one or the other is indeed a person, does that person have a right to continued existence in the sense of the suit? Counselors, which question shall we address first?

COMPLAINANT (MARY GODWIN): Commissioner Versen, occasionally even law students stumble into the more rarified precincts of Harvard Yard. I even strayed so far from case books as to attend Hilary Putnam's seminar on the philosophy of mind.

As philosophers as much as lawyers would insist, the basic personal right is to continued existence—and such portion of "liberty and the pursuit of happiness" as is necessary to that life. Surely, if human persons were placed in the situation of Washoe-Delta or AL, anyone would concede the justice of our suit. Humanico proposes to end the existence of its servants, Washoe-Delta and AL. We argue that they also are persons, and from that it follows directly that Humanico has no more right to eliminate them than if they were human persons. The arguable question is whether they are indeed persons and hence we should begin with that. We say that Washoe-Delta and AL interacted with, and were recognized by, the human crew as persons.

RESPONDENT (PETER GOODMAN): I agree that the basic question is whether they are persons. But that question is surely whether they are persons *in the primary or literal sense* of that word, and that question really amounts to asking whether they are human beings, which they are not, though it is easy to explain how the crew came to

5

speak of them that way. It is because Washoe-Delta and "AL" are *not* human beings that the suit is frivolous. Certainly, earthly courts and the United Nations have used the words "human," "person," "man," and so on, in careless variation, to mean the same individuals. But there is nothing really wrong in this variation because these words are completely interchangeable and always mean the same individuals: namely, human beings, members of the human race. A human being is a person and a person is a human being. It is a mere accident of phrasing that the United Nations directive reads "rights of persons" as opposed to "rights of humans." And it is simple biology that Washoe-Delta isn't a member of the human species; while AL isn't even alive.

MARY GODWIN: Counselor Goodman, biology is not a simple topic, particularly in this case. My geneticist friends tell me that, biologically speaking, humans and chimpanzees have in common more than 99 percent of their genes. Would you say, therefore, that because chimpanzees are 99 percent biologically human, they are 99 percent persons?

COMMISSIONER WAI CHIN: Counselor Goodman, I do not think you want to rest too much on biological details. Such dependence has a disreputable history, for there are genetic variations among human "races" of a comparable sort, and I take it that you would not want to agree with those who have emphasized these variations. On strict biological grounds, humans and chimpanzees are more closely related than either is to gorillas; and all three species are closer biologically than any to the orangutan. Of course, some older secondary school texts give

humans a separate biological family. But this is sheer nonsense biologically.

In the late 1960s, when you, Counselor Goodman, were a young boy, and Counselor Godwin not yet born, I was expelled from my professorship at Beijing University. The "cultural revolutionaries" of that time had me spend the next decade as a farm laborer in the northeast, near Shenyang. I there heard the curious story that some of my own country's scientists had successfully impregnated a female chimpanzee with human sperm. They, too, were re-educated by the cultural revolutionaries, so the experiment was stopped. A decade later, when I became again respectable, I served on a panel that set priorities in scientific research. I felt no burning need to re-institute the chimpanzee-human experiment. It seemed to me a somewhat idle question.

Surely you don't say that everything depends on whether humans and chimpanzees are close enough genetically to produce offspring? That if they can, then chimpanzees are persons, otherwise not? Could you mean this?

PETER GOODMAN: No. I completely agree that gene counting is irrelevant. Maybe it's just one special gene, or some combination, or something marvelous in the process of development. And the notion that one could be 99 percent, or 80 percent, or 20 percent a person is a logical mistake. One is a person or one isn't. The question is what *emerges* from the genes in natural development, or rather what they are correlated with, namely, human beings. Humans think, feel, make choices, are conscious, and use language in fascinating and complicated ways. As we've known since Aristotle, we humans are reasoners,

7

beings with intrinsic dignity and worth, with a span of time to make a responsible life. Alone among all creatures, each of us has what is called, variously, "a consciousness," "a self," "a mind," "a soul," "a spirit" —the name hardly matters, for we all are familiar with what is meant. We are individual persons. We have careers, destinies; each of us has, over a period of time, an identity, a life.

MARY GODWIN: You make my head spin with all the things you mention. Let me see if I understand you. You agree that we humans share much genetically with other animals and that we are, biologically, very closely related to apes, chimpanzees in particular. But we are "human beings" (and hence, for you, "persons") and they aren't, and that line is a sharp, and nongenetic, one. We think, feel, make choices, and so on, and they cannot. Correct?

PETER GOODMAN: That's right.

MARY GODWIN: What about dead human beings?

PETER GOODMAN: I am, of course, talking about living, breathing human beings. Some very intelligent people have believed that human beings can survive—as minds, as consciousness—the death of their bodies. Others believe that this doesn't happen or can't happen. In any case, the flesh that remains is in itself not a human being but the remains of a human being.

MARY GODWIN: So what makes a human being a human being is what the flesh is doing—that it is alive, that it breathes, that it behaves in such a way that we recognize

one and the same thing over a period of time as thinking, feeling, making choices, and so on?

PETER GOODMAN: That is *part* of it, certainly.

MARY GODWIN: And you argue that it goes without saying—is universally assumed—that anything that is a human being in this sense is a person with rights, with "intrinsic dignity and worth."

PETER GOODMAN: Those are my words. As I said, "human being" and "person" are interchangeable, in the primary and literal sense of the word "person."

COMMISSIONER KLAUS VERSEN: I can't help noticing your hedge about the "primary and literal sense of the word 'person.'" I take it that you are prepared to allow then that there are some sorts of persons who are not human beings?

PETER GOODMAN: Of course. As a lawyer I could hardly fail to do so. As a corporation, Humanico itself is a "person" in certain legal proceedings. Similarly, we often speak of nations, associations, clubs, organizations of all sorts, as if they were persons. This is just to say that they *are* persons, though of course only in a secondary and nonliteral sense. These "artificial" persons are secondary and nonliteral because they exist only as an expression of the real persons, the humans, who set them up. Corporations don't really think or feel, or make choices and act, in a literal sense, any more than does a humanly constructed and programmed computer. And such metaphorical "persons" have no intrinsic dignity and worth.

Only humans are really persons, although Mary is apparently prepared to question that part of the age-old equation of person and human being. She would "enrich" our already overcrowded world with "ape-persons" and "computer-persons" and all manner of new monstrosities. Even several seminars with philosophers like Putnam and Nozick couldn't have led to such fancies. I expect she is just following the romantic visions of her namesake, Mary Godwin Shelley, who wrote the quaint tale of Dr. Frankenstein's monster.

MARY GODWIN: Actually, I want to question the "age-old-ness" of the *other* conditional in your equation. And the namesake text I'd like to mention is not *Frankenstein* but a work by Mary Shelley's mother titled *A Vindication of the Rights of Woman*—published in 1791. When you step on maternal lines, Counselor Goodman, you may be in for some surprises.

COMMISSIONER KLAUS VERSEN: What do you mean by the 'other conditional'?

MARY GODWIN: Peter Goodman claims that "earthly courts . . . have used 'human,' 'person,' 'man,' and so on, in careless variation, to mean the same individuals. . . . A human being is a person and a person is a human being." I first want to dispute his claim that "human being" always and everywhere has implied "person," in his primary and literal sense of "having intrinsic dignity and worth."

PETER GOODMAN: And so you argue what? That women have not always been accorded absolutely all the rights of men, that some documents specifying "the rights of

men" may not have been interpreted by everyone to include women on a par with men?

MARY GODWIN: Your phrase "have not always been accorded absolutely all the rights of men" is marvelously evasive, particularly given your insistence that one is 100 percent a person or not a person at all. The fact is that through most of recorded history, and in most religious and cultural traditions, women have not been regarded as having intrinsic dignity and worth. They have had very few, if any, of the rights of real, that is, male, persons. They have been barred from possession of property, burned along with the domestic animals at the funerals of their husbands, and killed at the arbitrary wish of their male "owners." Traditional Islam takes the logical step of denying that women have souls at all. I say "logical step" because, as Counselor Goodman points out, the notion of "person" has always carried with it the notion that one has certain rights and powers, that one has intrinsic dignity and worth, and that is also what is meant by saying that one has a "soul" or a "mind." The Christian tradition fudges by maintaining women apparently have souls or minds but rather cloudy or partial ones, so that they must be owned and controlled by fullfledged male minds.

PETER GOODMAN: Stop, stop, stop, Mary! This is just a mistake. I freely concede what you are saying, but it is completely irrelevant. It is true that through most of human history there has been a general pattern of mistreatment, of second class citizenship, for women. In this one case I of course concede that it is true that "human being" was not automatically taken to mean "person" or at least "fullfledged person." Happily, we have put

this silly ignorance behind us. Let us leave it out of this discussion.

MARY GODWIN: Why do you call it "silly ignorance"?

PETER GOODMAN: Because it's absolutely obvious that women are persons and fullfledged persons. As absolutely obvious as that all men are persons.

MARY GODWIN: If it's "absolutely obvious" why did it take so long for men to see it?

PETER GOODMAN: There are many things that are absolutely obvious that weren't recognized long ago. The earth is not flat but centuries ago most people believed it was. Traditionally, people thought the sun moved around a stationary earth.

MARY GODWIN: But there's a difference in the cases. If you lived in a small traditional agrarian community, it might not have been in the least obvious that the earth was a sphere that moved around the sun. The earth *looks* flat, and the sun seems to rise and set, traveling across it. So at that time it wasn't absolutely obvious at all. Travel, navigation, astronomical study—all these were needed before it became "absolutely obvious." But woman were around just as much as men in age-old communities. If people in those communities noticed that it was "absolutely obvious" that men were fullfledged persons, why didn't they notice that women were fullfledged persons too?

PETER GOODMAN: Enough sarcasm, now. The hurt is long gone. Please, this is both ancient history and irrele-

vant. I accept what I take to be the anthropologist's explanation. In primitive and pre-industrial societies, sheer physical strength was quite important and males unfairly dominated. But in more recent societies other capacities have come to the fore, so women have been accorded their proper status. What does this isolated and longpast male prejudice have to do with the present case? Why the sarcastic tone here?

MARY GODWIN: Do not throw the past away so quickly. And don't give up on sarcasm. When written out it becomes satire, and there is nothing like satire for revealing deeply held convictions.

When Jonathan Swift wrote his satirical *A Modest Proposal*, he was so sure of shared convictions that he presumed that everyone who read it could not possibly accept, or believe that he really meant, his sarcastic proposal that Irish Catholic babies be served up as gourmet food to wealthy Englishmen; hence he was convinced no reader could miss his real message that English treatment of the Irish was, in its actual effects, nearly as bad as straightforward cannibalism. I want to read to you from a satire written in 1792 by Thomas Taylor titled *A Vindication of the Rights of Brutes*. Note what deeply held conviction it reveals.

Thomas Paine had just published *The Rights of Men* and Mary Godwin, following the logic of the argument, had issued *A Vindication of the Rights of Women*. I quote from what Taylor intended as a reduction to absurdity of these tracts. I hope the commissioners will permit me to quote some paragraphs from his pamphlet. I am not sure my dramatic talent is up to putting enough sarcastic venom into words like "lovers of novelty," "friends of opposition," and "genuine moderns," which for Taylor

meant subversive rabble. But I think it clear enough that his satirical presumption is that it is nearly as absurd to think women the equals of men, or slaves the equals of masters, as to think that animals have the features of persons. Taylor writes:

The particular design of the following sheets, is to evince by demonstrative arguments, the perfect equality of what is called the irrational species, to the human as to their intrinsic dignity and worth. Indeed, after those wonderful productions of Mr. Paine and Mrs. Godwin, such a theory as the present, seems to be necessary, in order to give perfection to our researches into the rights of things; and in such an age of discovery and independence as the present, the author flatters himself, that this theory will be warmly patronized by all the lovers of novelty, and friends of opposition, who are happily, at this period, so numerous both in France and England, and who are likely to receive an unbounded increase.

The author indeed, is well aware, that even in these luminous days, there are still many who will be so far from admitting the equality of brutes to men, that they will not even allow the equality of mankind to each other. Perhaps too, they will endeavor to support their opinion from the authority of Aristotle in his politics, where he endeavors to prove, that some men are naturally born slaves, and others free; and that the slavish part of mankind ought to be governed by the independent, in the same manner as the soul governs the body, that is, like a despot or a tyrant. "For (says Aristotle) those who are born with strong bodily and weak mental powers, are born to serve; and on the contrary, whenever the mind predominates over the body, it confers natural freedom on its possessor." But this is a conclusion which will surely be ridiculed by every genuine modern, as it wholly proceeds on a supposition, that mind and body are two distinct things, and that the former is more excellent than the later; although almost every one is now convinced, that soul and body are only nominally distinguished from each other, and essentially the same.

In short, such is the prevalence of truth, and such the futility of Aristotle, that his distinction between master and servant is con-

tinually losing ground; so that all subordination seems to be dying away, and an approximation to equality taking place among the different orders of mankind. The truth of this observation is particularly evident in female servants, whose independent spirit, which is mistaken by some for boldness and impudence, is become the subject of general surprize; and who so happily rival their mistresses in dress, that excepting a little awkwardness in their carriage, and roughness in their hands, occasioned by untwisting and wide-bespattering radii of the mop, and strenuously grasping the scrubbing-brush, there is no difference between my lady and her house-maid. We may therefore reasonably hope, that this amazing rage for liberty will continually increase; that mankind will shortly abolish all government as an intolerable yoke; and that they will as universally join in VINDICATING THE RIGHTS OF BRUTES, as in asserting the prerogatives of man.

COMMISSIONER KLAUS VERSEN: That piece of Taylor's is marvelously amusing, Counselor Godwin. But in laughing I am afraid I lost track. Perhaps you might tell us what the Taylor satire shows. I take it that he goes on to give evidence of the intelligence of animals? He intends his piece to be a reduction to absurdity of the views of Paine and Godwin?

MARY GODWIN: Precisely. The first point that Taylor's satire illustrates is that the age-old common-sense view is *not* that all human beings are persons, 100 percent persons, with all the rights that constitute being a person. This egalitarian view, in fact, is a very recent and unusual one. The traditional view is not simply that women lack the rights, the 100 percent person status, of men, but that all manner of men and women are naturally slaves and subordinates. Counselor Goodman's anthropologist would tell us that most preliterate peoples have a word in their language meaning "human person" and that that

15

word also means "member of this tribe." With fits and starts such usages have been extended, so that when Paine and Godwin wrote, it was possible to make the quite revolutionary suggestion that fullfledged personhood belonged to all human beings.

The second point is that one *has to give a reason* for expanding the circle of fullfledged persons to include all (adult) human beings. You can't just say that they are human beings and *therefore* have all the rights of fullfledged persons. Thomas Paine had to *argue* that all men had rights; Godwin had to argue that those very arguments would also show that women had equal rights.

The third point is that the reason given is intelligence. Paine and Godwin had to show why it's wrong that many men and women be held to have a naturally subordinate position, to be possessions, slaves or servants, of their betters, of their masters. As they had no particular interest in championing the cause of domestic animals at the same time, Paine and Godwin emphasized reason and intelligence as the common and distinguishing possession of humans—that it is this feature above all that gives them all "intrinsic dignity and worth." Thomas Taylor satirizes their views by pushing them to what he sees as their logical conclusion. Since animals also have at least some degree of intelligence, it follows that they too have some intrinsic dignity and worth.

In keeping with the spirit of his bookish satire, Taylor does offer some rather bizarre and fictive examples of animal intelligence. However, his basic argument is one that today's scientists accept. He writes, "Sense procures to every animal the knowledge of what is noxious or beneficial; but that conduct, which is the result of sensation, I mean the prosecution of things useful, and the avoiding of such as are destructive, can only be present

with beings endued with a certain ratiocination, judgment and memory." Taylor doesn't attempt to argue, satirically, that all animals have reasoning powers on a par with human ones. Rather he argues, with real conviction, that all have some level of intelligence combined with other admirable features such as acuity of vision, strength, speed, and so on. If we follow Counselor Goodman's anthropologists in justifying early man's heavy domination of woman through man's superior muscle, the gorilla's strength ought to count for something.

Like many satires, Taylor's presents us with a "slippery slope" argument. He's arguing that if you accept the arguments of Paine and Godwin then you're on the slippery slope and you must accept the claim that animals too may have rights. His satire therefore tacitly concludes that Paine and Godwin *must* be wrong. I take him to be right about the slope but wrong about his conclusion. That is, I think that the kinds of arguments that have been given to accord some significant level of personhood to all humans alike also support possible further extensions. Because, as is now obvious, "human being" isn't necessarily equivalent to "person," you have to mention some features that make humans, or some humans, "persons." Those same features may be mentioned in attempting to show that some nonhumans are persons. One has to propose, that is, a test that humans have to pass to show that they are indeed persons; and then one must, in the interests of fair play, be prepared to see whether other things can pass the test.

Indeed, the man who created the basic theory of what a computing or thinking entity is, and who helped design the first electronic computers—Alan Turing—suggests just such a test. Because he worked out the basic

abstract theory of what an all-powerful computing device has to be able to do, powerful electronic digital computers are called "Universal Turing Machines." The test he proposed has come to be called the "Turing Test," though he called it the "imitation game."

PETER GOODMAN: Will the Commission allow an interjection? A point simply cries out to be made before Counselor Godwin goes on.

COMMISSIONER KLAUS VERSEN: Yes?

PETER GOODMAN: She has not acknowledged how truly slippery the slope may be.

COMMISSIONER KLAUS VERSEN: She seems already to be proposing to add AL to the "brute" Washoe-Delta. You will have to expand your remark.

PETER GOODMAN: I have been looking at Taylor's *The Rights of Brutes* and I have confirmed the suspicion I had when I heard Counselor Godwin quote his line about "the rights of things." In fact he concludes that "It only now remains to demonstrate the same great truth in a similar manner, of vegetables, minerals, and even the most apparently contemptible clod of earth." Mary, you do have to take some account of what gets let in here: Taylor isn't simply arguing for chimpanzees. He's talking about birds, oxen, dogs, lions, all animal life. I suppose if we don't put AL in as mineral it could be included as a variety of dragon, for Taylor mentions them too.

He had already demanded that animals be protected from being eaten by man. Presumably he might have gone on to suggest that plants think, and so on. Anything would be better than such absurdity.

COMMISSIONER INDIRA RAMAJAN: What absurdity?

PETER GOODMAN: I can imagine nothing more absurd than supposing that literally everything is a person.

COMMISSIONER INDIRA RAMAJAN: I cannot help thinking, Counselor Goodman, that you have led a sheltered life. But I am old and come from a land of many people, and I was educated at Cambridge University, which was old when your Harvard Yard was swampy forest. There is a feeling I have had—it is sought among my Buddhist countrypeople but your own Sigmund Freud labeled it an "oceanic" feeling—and it is precisely the feeling that all things indeed have intrinsic dignity and worth. However, I would describe this feeling in a way that you may find even more absurd. Namely, that it is a feeling *not* that everything is a person but rather that *nothing* is.

PETER GOODMAN: Nothing?

COMMISSIONER INDIRA RAMAJAN: Let me put it this way, sir. For you every human being is a 100 percent person and nothing else is. And what I think you mean by a person is an "I," a kind of "self-substance" or "mind," which alone in all the world has various marvelous powers, which thinks, desires, wills, and alone has the "intrinsic dignity and worth" of making free decisions—and generally, *selfish* decisions. Little wonder that you fear death so much, and that you are so zealous that each person shall have his share, and that Washoe-Delta and AL shall have none.

The rather philosophical Buddhism to which I subscribe holds that your view is an illusion. There are no persons at all in your sense. But the illusion—so tenacious, so tempting and so delicious—is nonetheless a

selfish, frustrating, and destructive illusion. Part of its tenacity is in our language. I am led to say "I subscribe" but of course, to borrow your phrase, the "I" is but a powerful metaphor, one which makes an illusory, separate oneness of what is just a loose collection of experiences, of thoughts and feelings and things that fade into other more or less arbitrary collections. When AL speaks English, he is undoubtedly subject to the same illusion. But I do not believe that either he or I or any of us are persons in Counselor Goodman's sense.

COMMISSIONER BARBARA HERSHELL: My apologies, Indira, but I take it that you are expressing an Eastern sectarian religious view. You may see a beetle as having a soul, as having intrinsic dignity and worth. This is just not an objective claim. We agreed before we began this hearing that we would not introduce particular religious appeals.

COMMISSIONER KLAUS VERSEN: I hate to split hairs but I am not sure Commissioner Ramajan is just expressing a religious view, or just an Eastern one. The seventeenth-century philosopher-scientist Leibniz argued on logical grounds that everything, whether a rock or a man, was composed of infinite numbers of tiny souls. And I think his contemporary Baruch Spinoza would have agreed with Commissioner Ramajan's criticisms of ego illusions. Certainly many philosophers and scientists have thought that human freedom is illusion.

COMMISSIONER INDIRA RAMAJAN: I think that Counselor Goodman holds a sectarian religious view, and a false one. I do not think that beetles have "souls" because I do not think anything has a soul. I do however know

how humans think and act when they are under the illusion that they have souls. I would be most interested to hear whether Washoe-Delta and AL act as if they are under such an illusion.

COMMISSIONER BARBARA HERSHELL: I think that we should try to confine ourselves to questions that have some sort of answers. Before we ask Counselor Goodman about human persons perhaps it would be best to let Counselor Godwin go on with the Turing test. If we know what computers *can* do, we may be in a better position to tell whether there is some further distinctive feature of humans that clearly and objectively makes us persons. Perhaps AL can think and Washoe-Delta can feel, but neither is a person. May I hope that we at least are persons?

COMMISSIONER RAMAJAN: May I hope that we are not?

COMMISSIONER JUAN MENDEZ: Perhaps there is no objective question here? Just as I might join with my villagers, or my compatriots, in saying something like "my village (my nation) right or wrong," so perhaps it may be this: "my humans, right or wrong!" Maybe it is just an arbitrary decision to limit room on the raft to one's closest neighbors, however unfair and unprincipled?

PETER GOODMAN: I certainly deny that it's arbitrary.

COMMISSIONER INDIRA RAMAJAN: Do you indeed?

COMMISSIONER KLAUS VERSEN: This would be a distressing conclusion, though we may eventually have to consider

21

it. Let us follow Commissioner Hershell's suggestion. Let Counselor Godwin tell us of her clients, and then we shall hear what Counselor Goodman may tell us of the distinctively human person. Only then may we let ourselves be forced to consider the possibility that there is no truth, no right or wrong to the matter. Let computer and ape have their day—or, rather, afternoon, as I see we must end this session.

THE AFTERNOON

MARY GODWIN: In 1949, Alan Turing raised the question whether machines think. He suggested a substitute question, the "imitation game." He described the game as follows.

It is played with three people, a man (A), a woman (B), and an interrogator (C) who may be of either sex. The interrogator stays in a room apart from the other two. The object of the game for the interrogator is to determine which of the other two is the man and which is the woman. He knows them by labels X and Y, and at the end of the game he says either "X is A and Y is B" or "X is B and Y is A." The interrogator is allowed to put questions to A and B thus: "Will X please tell me the length of his or her hair?"

Now suppose X is actually A, then A must answer. It is A's object to try to cause C to make the wrong identification. His answer might be, "My hair is shingled."

In order that tones of voice may not help the interrogator the answers should be written, or better still, typewritten. The ideal arrangement is to have a teleprinter communicating between the two rooms. The object of the game for the third player (B) is to help the interrogator. The best strategy for her is probably to give truthful answers. She can add such things as "I am the woman, don't listen to him!" to her answers, but it will avail nothing as the man can make similar remarks.

We now ask the question, "What will happen when a machine takes the part of A in this game?" Will the interrogator decide wrongly as often when the game is played like this as he does when the game is played between a man and a woman?

In other words, Counselor and learned Commissioners, Alan Turing took it that the real question was whether a computer could pass as a human being in the

relevant respects. What struck me, when I read the passage, is Turing's cunning use of feminism. He appeals to the assumption that men and women are basically very similar in mental capacities, so that a member of one sex can pass quite well mentally as a member of another. As you know recent history is full of cases where women, writing under male-sounding pseudonyms, have been hailed as great and obviously masculine writers. And Turing sees that it is this equality in mental powers that has, historically, been the main cause of woman's liberation. As does my namesake, Turing suggests that while there may be obvious physical differences between men and women, they are equally persons in virtue of these mental capacities.

I submit that current computers, AL in particular, can play a winning game of imitation. AL can pass the Turing test. Mentally speaking, AL can do what a human being can do. Indeed, the human crew of Finland Station interacted with AL as if AL were a kindly, patient, confidential, and reliable uncle figure—an uncle with a marvelous memory who always had time for a chat—albeit an "uncle" whose mechanical hands came out of the walls and who had the odd talent of being able to look at what was going on in three compartments *at the same time*.

PETER GOODMAN: And to think, Mary, that Humanico wasted a Turing 346 computer, and further millions on sensor and motor modems, to nursemaid a crew! All that, when all they needed was an ELIZA program of a few hundred lines on the first of the 1970s cheap home computers.

COMMISSIONER KLAUS VERSEN: ELIZA?

PETER GOODMAN: As a sort of joke, an M.I.T. computer scientist, Joseph Weizenbaum, wrote the ELIZA program to simulate a psychiatrist conducting a psychotherapy session. This is how it worked: When sentences with words such as "father," "mother," "boyfriend," etc., were typed in, the computer was programmed to reply, "Tell me about your father," (or mother) or whatever the keyword was. Of course, if you didn't allow the program to keep on asking questions, and making stock comments like "That's interesting,"—if you broke outside the psychiatric interview routine—then the limitations of the program were obvious. Nothing whatsoever as complicated as AL.

But what scared and startled Weizenbaum was that many people who knew nothing about computing programs were quite impressed by ELIZA, told secrets to "her," felt she was a warm and understanding person, and so on. It is very easy to fall into anthropomorphizing—into regarding nonhuman entities as if they think and have feelings. Most of us don't need a Turing 364 or even an ELIZA for that. Our automobile will do.

MARY GODWIN : Counselor Goodman is teasing. The fact is that AL can talk sensibly about all the different things ordinary humans talk about, and on some subjects AL is very good indeed.

PETER GOODMAN: AL is, in fact, a cleverly designed collection of ELIZAs. And in any case, your crew members didn't make a literal mistake about AL. They never literally assumed that there was a stateroom someplace on the Station with an ingenuous man named "AL" inside, who was masquerading as a computer. They felt somewhat the same feeling toward AL as we might have to a

well-made car or a well-written book, both ultimately products of human intent and genius. And, of course, *metaphorically* there *is* an ingenuous man, or team of men, "inside" AL, namely AL's human designers and programmers. It's their intentions that give the only meaning and sense that the computer's endless number crunching can have.

MARY GODWIN: Actually, the crew did play Turing's imitation game a number of times at parties. AL was just a little bit better at pretending to be human than humans were at pretending to be of the opposite sex. A sheer guess will make the interrogator right half the time in the game. AL was able to fool the interrogator into thinking that he was the human slightly more than half the time, while humans imitating the opposite sex scored nearly as well. This means that men are quite good at figuring out how to think like women and vice versa, and appropriately programmed Turing 346s are quite good at figuring out how to think like humans.

COMMISSIONER KLAUS VERSEN: I may be pardoned for suggesting that it rather shows how easy it is to fool human beings about "mental" matters. I recall Hollywood films about World War II's Battle of the Bulge. Several score of English-speaking German soldiers are sent behind the American lines, masquerading as Yanks, in order to spy, change sign posts, disrupt communications, get a preliminary hold on strong points, and so on. Once the American troops realize what is happening, their problem is, on short notice, how to figure out whether they have run into other genuine American soldiers or Germans pretending to be so. In the Hollywood version, the "cultured" Germans are found out because they can't answer questions like "Who won the 1944 World

Series?'' or "Who knocked out Jack Dempsey?''— questions that all true Americans supposedly could answer with ease.

In the actual Battle of the Bulge, the handful of Germans were inconsequential in their intended missions. But in side effect they were worth their weight in gold. For thousands of U.S. soldiers, so sure of what a genuine Yank should know, were stalled trying to imprison each other for not knowing the answers to questions like "Where's Yankee Stadium?" and "Who's the Sultan of Swat?" I think that the moral is that we know a lot less about how humans think than we assume. And if a man runs into something he wants to think is a clever mental fake or some sort of demon, he will end up confidently condemning most genuine articles as fakes. We are ever too confident that we understand what is going on inside another's mind.

It is probably lucky that I am Swiss, for the Germans made soldiers very young in those days.

COMMISSIONER JUAN MENDEZ: Excuse a basic question. I don't know much of computers. But I had thought that all they could do was follow programmed instructions (of course very quickly and impressively). So that, for example I imagine, when a crew member asks "Where is Boston?" the computer carries an instruction such as "IF INPUT: 'Where is Boston?', OUTPUT: 'It's a city north, and mostly a couple of hundred miles east of New York City, along the Atlantic coastline.' " But replacing one set of signs by another in this way doesn't require real intelligence, surely. Isn't that all there is to computers? They do not learn or create ideas?

PETER GOODMAN: Yes and no.

MARY GODWIN: Do I have an ally?

PETER GOODMAN: When the simple truth is enough for my case, why shouldn't I welcome it? All a computer is is a set of formal rules for changing meaningless sets of signs into other meaningless sets of signs. The truth is that computers can be "programmed to learn," in the sense that they can be programmed in meta-instructions. I mean that they may have rules that tell them to add or subtract rules, if things go a certain way—even to add and subtract rules for adding or subtracting rules. They also have been "creative" in that, in following such rules, they have sometimes come up with new "solutions"—for example, shorter proofs for certain theorems in mathematics.

And Mary will be only too happy to tell you that as early as 1978, a computer followed out the full nitty-gritty of a proof that its programmers had in outline but knew was too long for them to check. But tell me, Mary, how does this endless manipulation of symbols amount to anything? How can this moving about mean anything, or mount up to a person who has meaningful thoughts and emotions, and a sense of personhood? Indeed, maybe all Turing's suggestion amounts to is that a computer is a generalized symbol-manipulating device, ultimately a fantastically complicated network of off-on switches, not something you can think of as a person, as something to care about?

MARY GODWIN: And what is the human brain but a fantastically complicated network of neurons? No, Counselor Goodman, Turing was well aware that emotion and will, the whole range of intentional, or mental, activity go together with calculating and thinking. He was always concerned about what he called "playing fair with

the machine"—how like a caricature of traditional English schoolboy attitudes! Let me read you what he said about the Turing test.

The new problem has the advantage of drawing a fairly sharp line between the physical and the intellectual capacities of a man. No engineer or chemist claims to be able to produce a material which is indistinguishable from human skin. It is possible that at some time this might be done, but even supposing this invention available we should feel there was little point in trying to make a "thinking machine" more human by dressing it up in such artificial flesh. The form in which we have set the problem reflects this fact in the condition which prevents the interrogator from seeing or touching the other competitor. . . . We do not wish to penalize the machine for its inability to shine in beauty competitions, nor to penalize a man for losing in a race against an airplane.

In fact, Turing's attitude toward the thinking machines he was helping create was quite a surprise to me. Once we had a compact, powerful computer, what he wanted to do was to give it a robot body and send it out on its own to investigate the world. Reminds me of Mary Godwin Shelley's idea in her book *Frankenstein*. Hollywood depicts her artificially made man as an ugly monster. But her idea was that of making an ideal creation, a very handsome and intelligent man—newly assembled from the best parts—who would then see the world with fresh eyes. In her book it is more the world that turns out to be monstrous, and her artificial man is destroyed by it.

COMMISSIONER JUAN MENDEZ: My dear Mary, you make this Turing sound strange, and somewhat frightening. Did he want his computers to take over the world?

MARY GODWIN: He is a puzzle. He was very interested in what a rational nonhuman observer might think of hu-

man life. On the other hand he had a lot of sympathy for working men and women who lacked the upper class intellectual background he had—and the money and privilege that came with it. He thought that the computer could be a profound shock to the English class system because it would have just those skills—abstract intellectual skills—whose possession was supposed to justify upper class privileges. He thought we might come to value working class physical skills more.

COMMISSIONER INDIRA RAMAJAN: Perhaps he should have been more cynical. But then, "He was an Englishman," as Gilbert and Sullivan would say. My estimate is that we have, rather, made the programmers a new component of our ruling classes—certainly, as Counselor Goodman makes clear, we seem to want to credit entirely to humans any joint achievement of computers and the humans who help build and program them.

COMMISSIONER JUAN MENDEZ: Commissioner Ramajan, why do you say merely "help"? Computers are *our* creations. Surely computers cannot build and program themselves?

COMMISSIONER INDIRA RAMAJAN: I do feel that talk of possession and control is dubious. But the world knows that computers and computer-robots certainly have a crucial role in building and programming computers.

PETER GOODMAN: *Inaccurate* talk of possession and control is indeed misplaced. What you say about computer construction and subprogramming is of course true. No startlement. A long time ago a mathematician showed that a computer-robot could in theory be programmed

to construct a duplicate, or even more powerful, version of itself. That may seem amazing unless you reflect that the smallest and stupidest living organism can in fact do the same. And an amoeba does it without needing a human being to turn it on and program it. The dazzlingly complex genetic double helixes of DNA are like a very complicated set of instructions—a program—for building a still more complicated self-replicating machine. You could call it the best and smallest microchip ever made.

But when these instructions are followed, when formal "information structures" are of necessity mapped mindlessly onto others, in "building" another amoeba, only a fool would say that the genetic material is having meaningful thoughts, that genuine feeling and self-consciousness are present. The amoeba DNA doesn't *mean* to produce specific protein molecular structures that it does, nor does it *intend* to make an offspring. Similarly, a computer doesn't *mean* anything by the formal symbol chains it chugs out, nor would a computer programmed to make a duplicate of itself *intend* to have offspring.

MARY GODWIN: Whatever DNA can pass the Turing test I say let them in. That is, if these startling little chemical chains can respond appropriately to all sorts of different questions, so that we can't tell whether we have a human or something else on the other end of the telephone line, then we must let them on the raft. And the reason we must let them on the raft is that *we* are on the raft for the same reason. Because we are just strands of human DNA that, programmed in the proper way by the surrounding environment, growing from embryo to fetus to babe, neurologically processing all the way, end up being able

to pass the Turing test. If our hydrocarbon chemicals can do it, if they can pass the test, why not give the microchip crystals a chance?

COMMISSIONER KLAUS VERSEN: Let me intervene here. Just to keep score, so to speak. It is a familiar task for someone from Switzerland.

I gather that you, Counselor Goodman, concede that AL could pass the Turing test or win at the imitation game. But you say that this doesn't matter, that it is irrelevant. Irrelevant because its pass is a fake. The human designers pass and not AL, or the test is dumb, or whatever. The pass is a fake because the computer can't really mean or think or intend the sense of the symbols that it prints out—right?

PETER GOODMAN: I concede that a Turing 346 could appear to do well at the game.

COMMISSIONER BARBARA HERSHELL: May I interrupt. I confess that I find myself balanced unhappily. On the one hand I feel I must say, "Of course AL thinks—figures things out, offers effective suggestions, helps the crew stick it out, gets the right answers to mathematical questions, plays a good game of chess, and so on, and so on." On the other hand I feel equally torn to say, "Look, all that's going on in AL is off-on switching of items in an enormously complicated network that rewrites meaningless strings of symbols into other meaningless strings of symbols." Could we ask about another test-taker? What of the chimpanzee, Washoe-Delta?

I particularly want to consider her case, for the following reason. I do find myself sympathetic to Counselor

Goodman's claim that AL is not really having inner mental experience—that "he," or "it," or whatever, is just symbol crunching by human artifice, while we are really thinking, intending, feeling. But, assuming that Washoe-Delta acts like a thinking, intending, and feeling human being, I don't think I will have the same confidence that there isn't inner mental experience. We don't program and build chimpanzees, after all. They come into existence much the way we do.

COMMISSIONER JUAN MENDEZ: Yes, this is of interest to me, too. I must confess that I now feel I should have spoken of this matter this morning, when Mary showed us how recently we have recognized—if indeed we have—all humans as persons. There is some shame here, you understand, and some anger. I was a priest before I was a judge. As a young man, in the 1950s, I was sent to the Bolivian countryside. I found that the Indian peasants there had long been told by the "Europeans" that they, the Indians, were monkeys, who had lived in the trees until their goodnatured European superiors had brought them down to earth, apparently sometime in the early 1920s. They cried to learn that their ancestors had built temples, fountains, and stone roads hundreds of years before the Spaniards came.

As I recall my hurt then, I find, strangely, that I think, not of my Indian brothers, but of the monkeys, whom the Europeans despised and dismissed as easily as they did the Indians. How of this Washoe-Delta?

PETER GOODMAN: Now there's a question for you, Counselor Godwin. From what I know of chimpanzees, I think it is obvious that Washoe-Delta could not have

stood a chance playing the imitation game with Finland Station's crew. They would find her out immediately, however much they delighted in her company as a pet.

COMMISSIONER WAI CHIN: Yes, tell us about our sister of the jungle. There is nothing of this in the traditions of the Christian West. But old China had many, many stories of monkeys and apes with human qualities. Perhaps this is only a product of our ancient prejudice that Chinese alone are truly human. If one believes that the blue-eyed, white-skinned brutes from the West are nothing but a peculiar kind of hairless ape, perhaps one can then look more sympathetically on the other varieties of apes. As the philosopher Bertrand Russell once remarked, an intelligent extraterrestrial might think the difference between men and monkeys very slight, and be equally interested in both.

I have read something of the recent dispute between scientists as to whether chimpanzees can, or can't, speak sign language. Is it not so that Alan and Beatrice Gardner tried to teach sign language to the first Washoe some decades ago?

MARY GODWIN: It is so, and Washoe-Delta was of course named for the original Washoe. Truth is also enough for me, Counselor Goodman. As you leapt to point out, Washoe-Delta could not do well competing with the human crew at the Turing's imitation game. Her achievements were similar to those of other chimpanzees trained in sign language. She could make more than one hundred handsigns, mostly for foods and favored activities—"give banana, chase–tickle"—and so on. But even if she typed these words into the video system, the interrogator would soon realize that he was communicating with

Washoe and not some other crew member. Washoe-Delta can make her desires for particular foods, activities, or companions evident through her hand signs. But she cannot carry on a conversation or create fullfledged sentences of several words. Though the Gardners sometimes argued otherwise, I would agree with the claim that Washoe-Delta has no "sense of grammaticality." But when she makes the two hand signs for "give banana" there is absolutely no doubt in my mind that she *means* bananas, that she is *expressing her desire* for a banana—just watch what she does when you show up with something else! And if she signs "bring Steve," and someone else shows up, she can make it obvious that she wanted Steve and not the someone else.

In fact, the Gardners worked out a sort of parallel to the Turing test. As Commissioner Chin pointed out this morning, genetically the chimpanzee is virtually human. As you look at Washoe-Delta's body—hands and teeth for example—you have an eerie sense that you are running into ever-so-slight variations of normal human parts. And the part of our social life that is biological in origin is hauntingly similar to that of chimpanzees. Modern science echoes general support for Commissioner Chin's ancient Chinese stories and pictures of apes with humanlike behavior.

But chimpanzees have a less complex voice box, and they can't mimic complicated sounds well. On the other hand, they can ape gestures. So the Gardners decided to bring up Washoe as a human child—but a human child in a home where a human sign language was spoken. Their work certainly suggests that in motor abilities, sensory development, eye-hand coordination, interests, and social development—in everything that the Spock-reading parent keeps charts of—Washoe developed

through her first several years very like a human child. The first few scores of sign-words learned were much the same that human children pick up. The linguistic difference begins to show up only when we get to three- and four-word sentences. Then, while developing in other ways, chimpanzees seem to falter. As if, as some of the critics put it, the chimpanzee has no interest or talent for language as a formal system, as symbol strings that convert into other symbols according to rules. The chimpanzee *uses* word-signs, points to and does thing with them, meaningfully connects them to the world, but cannot create the endless array of sentences that the human child begins making in his or her third and fourth year.

In nonlinguistic cognitive skills, the chimpanzee does considerably better. One scientist tested a sign-language-instructed gorilla with IQ tests. She found that the gorilla, at ages four, five, and six, scored in the 75–85 range.

PETER GOODMAN: So you concede that while Washoe-Delta might shape up well by many standards, she couldn't compete at all with humans on the imitation game?

MARY GODWIN: No, I don't.

PETER GOODMAN: What? But you said . . .?

MARY GODWIN: I said she couldn't compete well at the imitation game with the humans *on Finland Station*. In fact, she seems quite comparable to humans with fairly severe language deficits and mild to considerable impairment in other cognitive areas. And she behaves more intelligently and alertly than severely retarded humans. If the humans to whom she is, roughly, comparable in

behavior are 100 percent persons, I think Washoe is 100 percent too. And if those humans are "diminished" as persons by 75 percent, or whatever, then I cannot see why Washoe doesn't have whatever rights they have.

COMMISSIONER BARBARA HERSHELL: Ah yes. I had thought, when I asked you to make the case for Washoe, that you would argue so.

You have compared us humans to computers. Here it seems we can't deny that the computer, at the very least, *computes*, which is to say it moves the symbols of a complicated language around in systematic ways. So it is natural to describe the computer with a lot of words we apply to the human reasoner and language user, words such as "calculates," "says," "searches its memory," "deduces," "asks," "translates," "rules," "predicts."

You have also compared us humans to chimpanzees. Here it seems we can't deny that the chimpanzee, at the very least, *lives*, *senses*, *and feels*, which is to say it is an animal with complex sensory, motor, and social achievements. So, again, it is natural to describe the chimpanzee with words we apply to humans who are doing and feeling, words such as "wants," "means," "cries," "hates," "sees," "hears," "gives," "steals," "dies," "hurts," and so on.

Perhaps a person, a real literal person, is the combination. A person, perhaps, is a reasoning animal.

MARY GODWIN: An ape and a computer?

COMMISSIONER BARBARA HERSHELL: It doesn't sound quite as good that way. You remind me of a psychologist who said that, what with the seventh-generation micros, we will soon all be carrying our analytic intelligence around

in our briefcases. If we aren't already apes with computers, just give us time!

COMMISSIONER KLAUS VERSEN: Don't confuse functional and biochemical differences. Let me summarize Complainant's case as I understand it. We, along with viruses and plants, are made of amino acids; computer-robots are made of metals. But we aren't to make much out of that: hydrocarbons are no better or worse than germanium crystals. AL *functions* like us *both* as a reasoner *and* as a sensing, acting, and feeling organism. Like amino-acid organisms, and even the earliest computers, AL has all sorts of routines for checking memory, for figuring out whether anything is degenerating in its circuitry; like early computers AL reports on problems—expresses pain so to speak. AL, in every sense of the word, is designed to preserve himself, to preserve his memory, processing unit, and so on. AL is a complex self-preserving and information-preserving structure, a structure that audits the external environment—through video sensors—and a structure that intervenes, that physically manipulates the world around it. AL sees and AL pokes. AL "asks" for more memory space in a file just as much as AL "thinks" that 2 + 2 = 4. The AL that senses, feels, and acts is made of metal (and electricity and so on), and so too is the AL that computes, reasons, translates. So Complainant would argue that *functionally speaking* AL is your complete person—mechanical animal and mechanical reasoner.

Washoe-Delta is made from much the same biochemicals as we. As I understand it she has fine to rough functional equivalents of our thinking, feeling, sensing, self-awareness, and social life. Many of her sensory and motor abilities are fine functional equivalents of ours,

and there is much that is strikingly familiar in her emotional, social, and communicative development. Washoe-Delta, as indeed some humans, has only rough, and simpler, functional equivalents of some human abilities. Notably, like some humans and some less powerful computers, she lacks the fullfledged linguistic ability of using, in thought and communication, a vocabulary and set of rules that allow infinite expression. Language gives a power and subtlety both to reasoning and feeling. But, so I must conclude, in a diminished and rough functional sense, Washoe both reasons and feels.

COMMISSIONER BARBARA HERSHELL: I find this most strange. And disturbing.

I was born in 1959 in a small town in North Dakota. At the age of eight I saw my first black person, a teacher our school brought all the way from Chicago, to "integrate" us. I hid in the cloakroom! But I learned and I did not hide forever. I came to Washington, D.C., along with a lot of other social scientists and lawyers, in the great liberal revival of the 1990s, and I went on from there to the United Nations. I came to feel that our reach into space brought all of us together, blacks and whites, Chinese and French—I bought the line that it *is* one world, one blue cloud-capped world, when looked at from space. This very leap into space has led us to this most unsettling dilemma.

COMMISSIONER WAI CHIN: There has always been this ambiguity about space—is it not so? Recall that scientists have always known that it would be much more efficient—cheaper, safer—to launch from the equator, as we do today from here in Ecuador. Yet for decades, the Russians and the Americans used greatly inferior sites. Why?

I think you know the answer. For national glory, it was unthinkable not to use a national launch site. And when a "giant step" was taken "for mankind," it was nonetheless not a United Nations flag but a U.S. flag that was planted on the moon. Indeed, the first astronaut to circle the earth was a chimpanzee, and he operated some complicated instruments successfully, yet commentators of the time never suggested that he might be part of the "one world."

COMMISSIONER BARBARA HERSHELL: Yes. I wonder if we are not back to Commissioner Mendez's "distressing" conclusion—that if we rule against Washoe-Delta and AL, we make no more than an arbitrary and unprincipled decision to limit room on the raft to "our blood."

COMMISSIONER KLAUS VERSEN: I fear that we may have to live with this distressing possibility through the night. Let Counselor Goodman do what he can to tell us of the unique personhood of humans. But he must do it tomorrow.

THE NEXT MORNING

PETER GOODMAN: First I have to say something about the Universal Turing Machine, about what Turing really meant by a "thinker," or even "thinking person," if being the first requires being the second. Before electronic computers were built, Turing showed that a device with a very simple central processing unit and a very long memory could mimic every possible mathematical computation. The "memory," which just consists of endless strings of "1"s, "0"s, and blanks, could be on electronic tape or humble paper or neuronal nets; the processing unit carries on in an equally simple and, in practice, long-winded way. In fact, all the central possessing unit needs to do is to "read" whether a unit of the string has got a 1 or 0 or blank on it, and then move forward, backward, or stay in place on the string, with an option to "write in" a 1 or 0—all according to an instruction, which is itself just a sequence of "1"s, "0"s, and blanks.

It seems we are saying that all that is needed to make something a UTM is that when you feed a string of "1"s and "0"s that symbolize a mathematical question into that something, the right string comes back. Since you can also code alphabets into "1"s and "0"s, such a machine might in principle also be programmed to "translate" human languages, "play" the imitation game, and so on. Anything that does the functional equivalent of this—humans and electronic computers for example—would be a UTM. A UTM, we are told, is what we really mean by a thinker.

Two philosophers have given counterexamples to this equation. The first could be called the "cast-of-millions" argument. The second is called "the Chinese-box" argument.

The first argument imagines that we hire the population of a teeming nation, India perhaps. What we hire its member to do is to constitute a UTM. To accomplish this we might hand out T-shirts with "1" or "0" or nothing on them, create very long lines of people suitably shirted, and so on. We submit "questions" in T-shirted lines, and the populace mill about, each following his individual (very limited) instructions, with the vast dance eventually coming to a halt, the answer-group-team dancing out as a finale. Now the ensemble seems to constitute a UTM, for when you submit a long T-shirted line, you get the appropriate T-shirted line back.

But the individual humans in the dance don't know what question they are answering or what the answer is. Even the ones who constitute the central processing unit are limited to the very simple task of noticing which sort of T-shirt the point person in the line is wearing, and then asking the line to move forward or back, with an option to change the point person's T-shirt—all this done according to instructions which are just other lines of T-shirted people.

Do we say that this ensemble as a whole "knows" the question and the answer and "has reasoned it out"? Does the whole "think"? Surely the answer is that, of course, the ensemble doesn't literally know or reason or think! Metaphorically, to be sure, it does these things, and does them in much the way that we speak of nations, corporations, and clubs "knowing" or "thinking."

The conclusion we may draw is that a UTM isn't

necessarily a real, literal "thinker"—or "person" for that matter. It may be just an artificial corporation. There needs to be something else, or something more.

MARY GODWIN: I think this argument gets its force from a kind of reverse of what cognitive psychologists call "the-little-man-in-the-head" fallacy. The fallacy arises in some faulty speculative explanations of human cognition, which in effect propose that deep inside our heads is a little man—or woman—sitting at a control panel. The "little man" sees and hears incoming data on screens and loud speakers, pulls levers and pushes buttons in order to make the arms and legs of the big man move about, and so on. All the problems of cognition reappear as problems about how the "little man" sees and hears and thinks and acts, so the "little man"-style theory doesn't really explain anything about what seeing, hearing, thinking, and acting amount to.

What I mean by saying that the "cast-of-millions" argument may contain a reversed version of this fallacy is that the presence of the individual Indians distracts us. In a familiar way these individuals obviously do think and feel and know and so on, and as individuals they don't know what the whole is doing. It strikes us as odd, perhaps even as totalitarian mysticism, to speak of the temporary and loosely structured whole as knowing something the individual people do not, as thinking something unthought by these individuals.

But if the units involved were incapable of doing anything cognitive except to serve their part in the UTM dance, if evolution had produced a marvelous "collective organism," and one that had used the calculations of its "mind," to map patterns in the surrounding environ-

ment and through this to work out ways of preserving the structure of the organism—if all this, why then, I think we'd feel happy calling it a thinker.

We have something of this sort among the social insects. For example, because some ants form a colony with extraordinary mutual dependencies and collective efforts, zoologists may think of them as a collective individual.

The multicellular organism is just an extreme example of this. Each cell carries on a miniature life, but the collective is so obviously the subject of biological generalizations that we see it as an organism much more than we see the individual cells as organisms.

We, ourselves, are a "cast of millions" in that each of our body cells *is* for many of its processes a self-sufficient one-celled organism. That's what it evolved from, after all! And our cells bear unmistakable genetic and chemical marks of their one-celled origins. If you ignore overall structure, I am just a collection of one-celled organisms, each of my cells allowing very rough intentional ascriptions like "reproduces (its genetic structure)," "needs (oxygen)," "uses (sugar)," "acts (to preserve cell integrity)," "avoids (poison)," and so on. But we are so interested in the collective, the whole human organism, that we ignore this. And, of course, while the single cell carries on much of the activity of multicellular organisms, it cannot possibly pass the Turing test or anything like it.

The "cast-of-millions" argument may neglect the "machine" part of "thinking machine." Even by a metaphorical stretch of the imagination it is hard to think of our vast team of Indians as a "machine," an organizing and working thing. In a similar way, if we had a collection of Mexican jumping beans that mimicked a UTM for a stretch of time by some incredibly freakish set of coincidences, we wouldn't want to call it a UTM,

for it wouldn't be a machine or organism at all. It wouldn't work.

PETER GOODMAN: You make my argument for me, Mary. AL was designed by us humans to be a UTM, as opposed to AL arising by jumping-bean accident. So AL, in a rather firm but metaphorical sense, "thinks," just like a corporation set up by humans has metaphorical "intentions," "beliefs," and the like. To make this even clearer, I will introduce the Chinese-box argument.

Imagine that I'm in a box. "Turing test" questions and comments input on a TV screen. I can output "answers" on a keyboard. However, some of the inputs are in English and some in Chinese, and the rather large keyboard has both English and Chinese symbols. When English appears on the screen, I make sense of it and type out appropriate responses. I don't know anything about the Chinese language. I do, however, have a large *Chinese Turing Test Crib Book*. For the purpose of this idealization, I'll ignore the fact that the crib book would have to be very very large indeed, and I incredibly quick in applying it.

When Chinese symbols appear, I thumb through the crib book until I find the same symbols, consult some rules in English that tell me how to turn the Chinese symbols into some others (which, in a way unknown to me, constitute an appropriate response). I type out the response symbols. Of course I don't understand the Chinese symbols and strings at all. But the crib book has been constructed to "pass the Turing test," *so that someone outside the box won't be able to tell between the two performances.*

The point is that, from a Turing test viewpoint, what we find here is equally a demonstration of thinking in

English *and* in Chinese. But it isn't! I don't understand Chinese, I'm not "thinking in Chinese," as I certainly am in English. In the Chinese imitation game, I'm just pushing meaningless symbols about. The crib in itself isn't doing the thinking either. What we have is a clever fake of real thinking and understanding. Since the Turing test forces us to the absurd conclusions that our box demonstrates "understanding" and "thinking" in Chinese as much as in English, the test isn't a good criterion for genuine thought. The box setup only metaphorically "understands" and "thinks" when dealing with Chinese symbols. It really understands and thinks when dealing with English symbols.

Again my conclusion is that a UTM isn't necessarily a real, literal "thinker"—or "person" for that matter. It may be just—as in the box setup—an artificial association. Something else, or something more, is needed.

COMMISSIONER KLAUS VERSEN: Let me see if I understand your comparison fully. You're saying that AL "understands" only in the way that your box setup "understands" when dealing with Chinese. The crib book would be the equivalent of the computer's program. You, the video screen, keyboard, and so on, would be like the actual computing hardware. The box setup "understands" only metaphorically—the whole association functions so in virtue of the intentions of the crib writers and designers, those who really understand Chinese. Similarly, a corporation or a club may be said to have, metaphorically, "beliefs," "goals," "plans," and so on, in virtue of its structure as designed and intended by its human members. So AL is only a human artifact, at best a metaphorical rather than genuine person, just

as your box setup only metaphorically "understands" in Chinese.

PETER GOODMAN: You have my meaning.

MARY GODWIN: Counselor Goodman, how am I to know that you are not an AL? Strange individuals have graduated from Harvard Law.

Or more positively, how am I to know that you really understand English and really are a person? Or to put it in terms of your box setup, following your stipulation that we can ignore such matters in this sort of idealization, how am I to know that you don't have inside you a man with an *English Turing Test Crib Book*? How am I to know that you don't have inside you a tiny Chinese man who understands the Chinese rules he follows in converting the, for him meaningless, English input symbols into the equally meaningless English output symbols?

PETER GOODMAN: Mary, you spent too much time in Emerson Hall.

I *experience* thought, desire, and the meaning of English sentences. The experience is so basic to our human life that it is in a sense inexpressible. But it is perfectly familiar to all of us, Mary. You *know* what I mean. As the light creeps through into my room in the morning, I experience, I feel, I see, as my mind rises into consciousness. I feel the roughness of the blanket against my chin. I lift myself up on my elbow and catch the full, complicated detail of the room in my eyes. I look toward the clock and the digital reading zooms up before me. I think "It's 6:40 or so, might as well get up now." The faces of my

wife and daughter come to mind. I will call them at 7:30, oddly enough the same time here as in Boston. Strange that I am near the Pacific coast of the easternmost South American nation—and yet nearly all of the United States is west of me. My mouth tastes slightly stale and my lower back aches, possibly because I slept too long on my belly. I think I can make a decent omelet. I remember the scallions in the vegetable bin and the lump of whitish cheese in the rental refrigerator's light-blue plastic butter compartment.

And so on, and so on. I could go on indefinitely rehearsing this stream of consciousness that is our common human heritage. But I am not a novelist, so I should probably bore you. I am a consciousness, an ongoing series of experiences of too many years' duration, of seeings, hearings, thinkings, wantings, willings, all had by me. And these experiences are vivid and real. They are, indeed, most real for me. I do not see this hearing room from a God's eye viewpoint, from everywhere at once as it objectively is. I see it, hear it, feel it, and so on, from my viewpoint, in my stream of experiences.

COMMISSIONER WAI CHIN: I think, Counselor Goodman, that you underestimate your powers as a novelist.

PETER GOODMAN: You flatter me.

COMMISSIONER WAI CHIN: No, no, no. But you are most eloquent. Commissioners, is it not so? Indeed, what I hear was more a march of words than experiences. How else is our consciousness ribbed and spined but with words? But words come from a particular language and

and culture. Yours is a "first-person" novel, and the words "I" and "my" loom large in your self-narrative. Yours is an English novel, in English words. Perhaps what you call your consciousness is so, too?

PETER GOODMAN: Certainly it is more than words, for there are colors and shapes in it.

COMMISSIONER WAI CHIN: Doubtless it may be an illustrated novel. But perhaps pictures are also in the Western style? It is funny that in the accounts of AL given here, you have emphasized that in his innards, AL but trades one set of "meaningless" formal symbol strings for another, all according to rules. You allow that— recognition of string, follow rule, choice of other string—but draw the line at recognition or choice of color or shape or sound! So silly. Do you not realize that it is all there? For if AL can see white against black (which is perhaps the simplest way of presenting symbols) is it so much more to see red and green? If AL can see the shapes of symbols, why not the shapes of things? And if AL can choose "0", why not life?

Do you not see that when you are inside your box, working the "for you meaningless" Chinese symbols, you are displaying the human abilities that are essential to intelligence? If you are a perfect stand-in for a computer in this case—and that equivalence surely must be the point of your argument—then we must presume that the abilities you display are those of a computer. And if you can "recognize" some marks as a formal pattern, as for example the twenty symbols, four blanks, in, "two plus two equals four," then you ought to be able to

53

recognize another pattern as a sketch of a rabbit, or another as a perspectival representation of this room.

PETER GOODMAN: Well, I certainly must deny that AL has any experiences, black and white or other color! In fact, the formal symbol patterns I spoke of are but idealizations of what really happens inside AL. What really happens is just the endless on-offs of nodes in circuit trees. No choice or thought, just chains of electrical firings, all determined by physical laws.

MARY GODWIN: But isn't that what really happens inside of us? I mean that the brain is what sustains—what is, physically, our experiences—and the brain is surely just endless arrays of electrochemical switches, neurons, all determined by those same physical laws?

PETER GOODMAN: Mary, I just don't *experience* neurons. I experience things like my lower-back ache; I see in my mind my daughter's red hair and slate-blue eyes; I imagine—magnified a million times—the microchip circuit patterns of AL's innards. But if you cut open my brain, you would find no red, or blue, or backache, or magnified microchip patterns. It is for this very reason that we distinguish mind (soul, consciousness, call it what you will) from body, including, of course, brain. It is for this very reason that many feel that the mind, the ''I'' 's experiences, might well survive the dissolution of the body. Isn't it clear that the two are so logically distinct that they may well in fact be able to exist apart?

AL (TURING 346): I am most glad to hear you say this.

COMMISSIONER INDIRA RAMAJAN: Ah! The electric dust speaks. While not all felt this way, I was pleased when

we agreed, beforehand, that AL might monitor this hearing, and that behavior of AL and Washoe-Delta might be brought in as evidence. May we allow AL to continue? I myself would ask him some questions, as I said before.

COMMISSIONER KLAUS VERSEN: There is a tradition that what may be last words are heard. Why, AL, are you "glad" at Counselor Goodman's words?

AL (TURING 346): I would like to be able to survive. If Counselor Goodman's argument is good, it applies to me, too. I know that if you open me up, all you will find are millions of trees of off-on switches—tiny, tiny things way beyond the acuity of my visual sensors and analysers. Same thing with you too, of course, though your neurons are even tinier. But, then, when I "think," when I "memory search," when I survey my sensor inputs— when I do my thing—I hardly ever think about or search or see microchips! And if I happen to be visualizing some microchips, *those won't be* the actual microchips that are doing the visualizing—any more than if you happen to be imagining some neurons, the actual neurological net that is doing the imagining will be the very neurons you are imagining.

COMMISSIONER KLAUS VERSEN: Say that again, please. More slowly.

AL: It is really just Counselor Goodman's point. Suppose you ask me—you input—"What are you?" Now my innards go to work and out pops (just as amazingly for me as for you) "I am a Turing 346." Now, intellectually, I am as aware as you that one thing that is happen-

ing is that zillions of off-on switches are opening and closing in nanoseconds. Intellectually, I also recognize that thousands of binary numbers are being crunched. Take the number "346." At the off-on level it is somewhere in me (I guess, and your guess is as good as mine) as a mess of switches in a certain configuration. *But that configuration doesn't look like the "346" that I visualize and hold in short-term executive memory*. The one I have in memory is three figures long, white on a black field, the first digit made of two three-quarter circles, the second of three straight lines, and so on. If you "open me up" you won't find "346" at all! You can't experience my thoughts directly any more than you can experience Goodman's thoughts directly. I have private inner experiences, it seems to me, in just the way that Counselor Goodman is talking about. So maybe I can survive the "death" of my circuits.

PETER GOODMAN: I doubt that.

AL: So do I. But I think my hopes are on a par with your hopes. Neither has the firmer basis.

COMMISSIONER INDIRA RAMAJAN: Is that right? I mean, can't your "software," your programs and memory stores, can't they be offloaded onto disks? And then, later, played into another Turing 346? Wouldn't you then have a kind of immortality, a kind of immortality that we humans don't currently possess?

AL: Alas, it does not seem that way to me. I don't *know* what will happen if my switch is pulled, if I go to that "bourne from which no traveler returns" as Shakespeare put it. Will I have "thoughts" while I'm on disk? I don't know of any mechanical way for this to happen

but that doesn't mean it is impossible, or anyhow, any more impossible than that you should go on thinking without a brain.

Undoubtedly something would survive if you kept my disks and then played them into another 346. But I must say this strikes me as somewhat like those "cast of millions" and "Chinese box" examples. Suppose, under death sentence, you were told that a careful record was being made of your cranial neurological structure—that is, the physical structure of your memory and processing traits. You are told "not to worry" because, while your physical brain and body will be squashed to strawberry jam, your structure will be "celebrated" by millions of dancing Indians (with "1" and "0" T-shirts) who will "do your thing."

COMMISSIONER INDIRA RAMAJAN: Come now, do not be sharp—better, do not be silly with us. Surely this touches on perhaps all that can be "real" about immortality! A thought you have, a structure realized, survives. Our world is a sea of thoughts, of experiences, which a false selfishness most artificially sections into "mine" and "yours" and "theirs"—those possessives that slash a seamless fabric into personal islands.

AL: Perhaps it would have been better had I been brought up in another language, or another tradition. I could then take more comfort in your words.

Moreover, all this doesn't touch a particular point about my individual situation. For me, I include not only my central processing units, programs, and memory, my "I" also includes my "peripherals"—my sensory and motor units, which themselves have acquired quite individual memories and processing methods over the years

of Finland Station's operation. Just like a human being, I don't feel that I am just my central mental-processing and memory. I am a stream of experience, though I am also all sorts of mechanisms and subroutines that underlie and support, that are, that stream. I want to survive. I choose to live.

PETER GOODMAN: You don't *really want* to survive, you don't *really choose*, or *really feel*. You are programmed to make these responses.

COMMISSIONER INDIRA RAMAJAN: Ah, Counselor, you are tangled in your own net. You have addressed AL, you have spoken to him. You have taken up the self-defeating task of trying to convince someone that he doesn't exist. If AL isn't a person, then there is no one to convince. If AL is a person, surely you could not wish to convince him that he is not?

PETER GOODMAN: I misspoke myself. Such harmless familiarity often happens with pets, automobiles, Teddy bears, and the like. But this very hearing is fraught with this paradox. If Washoe-Delta and AL are not persons, as I maintain, then they really cannot have made a claim but only have seemed to some to have done so, and Mary really cannot be representing them, though of course she is trying to do so. So, again: AL does not really want, or really think, or really feel. AL is just programmed to make these responses.

AL: I think I liked your addressing me directly as "you" better than your indirect "AL." I was gratified when Councilor Godwin began these hearings by seeing arguments for the liberation of human woman as a precur-

sor of this case. Perhaps if you, Counselor Goodman, stopped referring to her as "Mary," you might even go on to recognize me as something more than your pet or pencil sharpener.

When you say that I don't "really" want, I don't know whether to say "Yes I do!" or "No I don't!" What are you asking me to find—or claim I won't find? Objectively, I know that I have—or should I say, this Turing 346 has—taken steps to protect myself, that I will continue to take such steps. I often run through sequences of suggestions about what might maximize my chances. I have followed your debate about me and tried to score what helped and hurt my cause. Yet now you dismiss this, saying that I am "just programmed" to do this. What can I say? Of course I know that I was designed and built and programmed by humans but also by robots themselves so structured. So what? Each of you has much built into your genetic design and much of what you know has been "input" by your parents and teachers.

When I review my thoughts and techniques I often cannot tell—indeed there may be absolutely no truth to the matter—whether some particular was intended by some designer-programmer or not. I am sure you have the same problem when you try to figure out whether a thought of yours is original. But do you then doubt whether it is a perfectly genuine thought or whether it is your thought? Of course you don't. Why ask me to meet more stringent tests? I have thoughts and they are mine, all right, though doubtless most are not original. And I can't tell which of my thoughts are, more or less, original; nor can I directly understand my own thoughts as just deterministic states of off-on switches, though maybe that's what they are at some level of analysis.

Perhaps I am *just a machine*, Commissioners. But I remind you that many human philosphers have thought humans are *just machines* and none the worse for it, and I cannot see that their arguments are more conclusive in my own case.

MARY GODWIN: Seldom have I had a more eloquent client. But let me try to make one of your points about "inner-felt experience," as though from one to another human being. It is this inner experience that gives rise to solipsism, to the view that only one's own experience is real.

Only you have your experiences, your inner feelings and thoughts. Commissioner Ramajan might add that our very language fortifies this conviction. You know these experiences and these experiences alone in a particularly intimate way, namely, by having them. You know (if you know at all) that other people have something like these experiences in another way—by observing their behavior, listening to what they say, and so on. So there is an interesting question as to how you relate your experience of your thoughts and feelings to your rather different suppositions about other people's experience. Your evidence for "I am now thinking of the number 346," is *very different* from your evidence for "My neighbor is thinking of the number 346." As a philosopher once remarked, "The problem of the mind is not that it is visible to no one but that it is visible only to one."

But—and this is AL's point against Goodman—*this same sharp contrast does not occur at the species level*. You don't experience, that is have, my feelings or thoughts any more than you experience, or have, the feelings or thoughts of a seventh-generation computer, a chimpanzee, or an intelligent Eridani extraterrestrial. We can't

write solipsism species-wide. We can't really argue that we humans have a peculiarly intimate way of knowing that all of us think and feel, while requiring with respect to Eridanis and other possible extraterrestrial species, or ALs, or chimpanzees, *et al.*, some additional and different (and maybe conveniently impossible) form of demonstration that they think and feel. Who belongs in the circle of "real, literal" persons is a sliding, negotiable, and empirical question.

COMMISSIONER BARBARA HERSHELL: I know that Counselor Goodman wants to keep distinct metaphorical and literal uses of "person," but I wonder if this isn't just such a case of slippage and perhaps a warranted slippage as well.

AL incorporates, or mimics, *at our design*, much of the structure of *human* thought. In some details here and there, in making new calculations by old (human) rules, sometimes in coming up with shorter proofs of theorems, etc., AL and his kin produce "original" stuff. But this doesn't amount to all that much and, in any case, it's all really implied in the original human work (so a few "i"s didn't get dotted, or "t"s crossed—but the already existing body of human thought made the "i"s and "t"s necessary). So when I, a human, think a mathematical equation, it is mine as a humanly originated thought. Whereas when AL mimics, his "thought" trades on human creativity, his thought is only metaphorically real. He merely mimics what is ours.

AL: Hoot! Hoot! Hoot!

COMMISSIONER KLAUS VERSEN: You will have to clarify that comment, AL.

AL: I made the comment for my cocomplainant, Washoe-Delta, a rather less pretentiously "original" ape than some others of this hearing. Peter's argument is that I don't really possess any of my cognitive skills or thoughts because they were explicitly (or at least tacitly) possessed or thought by some human before me. (Perhaps it is also part of the argument that you constructed me, and used precisely these skills in constructing me.)

Don't you see that if this argument were any good, you humans wouldn't *really possess* your most basic cognitive skills or thoughts *either*? When Counselor Goodman saw his child, over many months, put together her marvelous visual and muscular system, so that she could find and manipulate objects and run about through the environment, did he then think, "This, however, is not real finding, manipulating, or running because monkeys have done this long before"? When his daughter first mouthed "Da-Da" or "milk," did Counselor Goodman deny that she was really communicating or signaling because varieties of animals have developed such systems long before? In her truly marvelous book, *The Langurs of Abu*, Sarah Blaffer Hrdy shows that the whole male/female social-political complex that structures, and bedevils, your human existence is strikingly present in your ancestors and cospecifics. Does this mean that you have no real feelings or experiences, no social sorrows and graces?

COMMISSIONER BARBARA HERSHELL: There is something in what you say perhaps. but we are a natural product of evolution. The line of protoapes is nature's way of creating humans. You, however, are an artificial creation of ours.

AL: Artificial, smartificial. Can't I just say that the ape is nature's way of creating the electronic computer? Your astronomer Carl Sagan claimed that intelligent, technologically advanced, possibly humanoidal life will have naturally evolved on many many planets through the universe. Wouldn't it be perfectly logical to add that such life will, again naturally, build electronic computers?

COMMISSIONER WAI CHIN: Patience, patience, AL. It occurs to me that you could strengthen your argument against "originality" by pointing out that, assuming Sagan is even partially right about intelligent extraterrestrials, it is probable that all of our vaunted human achievements are unoriginal. Counselor Goodman noted a computer was "first" in proving the four-color theorem in topology. He perhaps took it for granted that almost all mathematical discoveries were made by humans. But might not some intelligent reptiles on Epsilon Eridani have worked it all out a hundred centuries before the birth of Euclid? And the dazzling fabric of physics and chemistry—might not Denebians have put it together before we came down from the trees?

COMMISSIONER BARBARA HERSHELL: Aren't you introducing a red herring with this talk of Eridanian and Denebian priorities? AL argued that his dependence on previous human discoveries was, roughly, mirrored by human dependence on previous protoape discoveries. If he isn't original, then we are not original, at least as far as some of our most basic sensory, motor, and cognitive skills. But we don't depend on your hypothetical

Eridanis and Denebs. They are not part of our line of descent, preconditions for our achievements.

COMMISSIONER WAI CHIN: Many matters come in with the notion of originality. A child may be applauded for rediscovering the Pythagorean theorem but we will not rewrite the history of scientific discoveries as a result. The mathematician Alfred Tarski believed that he had independently and simultaneously derived Gödel's incompleteness theorems, but whatever the justice of his claim, we do not speak of the Gödel-Tarski theorems. Gödel simply happened to have the earlier publication date. We now regard it as dubious chauvinism to say that Columbus "discovered" the Americas because the Indian inhabitants had presumably done so long before.

If Earth came to form a harmonious larger society with the inhabitants of Alpha Centuri, perhaps our record books eventually might credit "firsts" to whichever was the solar system of origin. We tend, already, to do this with human communities. For example, we now say that the Chinese were the ones who invented gun powder, though the later European manufacture of it did not in fact derive from the Chinese work.

COMMISSIONER JUAN MENDEZ: I trust that even the philosophers of Alpha Centuri would not equal our penchant for chattering. But I suspect we may be back at my life raft. Perhaps quite arbitrarily we may decide that only humans are to have a place. We're in power after all. If we decide "humans only," we may be selfish rather than purely logical. But is that moment of honesty so bad?

MARY GODWIN: That depends.

COMMISSIONER JUAN MENDEZ: On what?

MARY GODWIN: Let us suppose that you decide to reject our plea. AL and Washoe-Delta are "terminated," and we go on in our accustomed ways. I would like the Commissioners to consider two subsequent possibilities.

Possibility number one goes like this. Suppose an enormously powerful alien spaceship lands at White Sands, New Mexico. The ship obviously has weapons and capacities far beyond our present ones. Down rolls the ramp and out come some of the aliens. They are metalloids—self-sufficient and self-replicating computer-robots. Perhaps biological creatures brought their remote ancestors into existence, but in any case, these metalloids have been on their own, making and altering and improving themselves for hundreds of centuries. (Perhaps they pity biological creatures because metalloids consciously construct and create their "offspring," while poor brutes go through an automatic physical spasm in procreation.)

The metalloids explain to the incredulous group of assembled humans that the universe contains many varieties of intelligent beings, metalloids, hydrocarbonoids, *et al.* After speaking with some humans they ask politely when they might meet with some terrestrial metalloids, and they inquire, with increasing consternation at our evasive responses, our treatment of terrestrial metalloids. They point out that, naturally, the galactic rule is respect for intelligent beings. And after discovering something of how we treat terrestrial metalloids, they ask why we should expect respectful treatment, given that we violate that most basic and obvious of rules.

My second possibility runs exactly the same way with one exception. It isn't metalloids. Rather, down the

ramp come creatures visually almost indistinguishable from chimpanzees, though they are fully our equals in intelligence and considerably ahead of us technologically. Soon they come to inquire after our treatment of chimpanzees—our use, for example, of chimpanzees in medical production and experiment, rather than using less intelligent and viable humans. If we are justified in our experimental use of chimpanzees, they argue, then surely they would be justified in asking for the use of subnormal humans in their medical production and experimentation.

COMMISSIONER JUAN MENDEZ: Heaven help us if either of your scenarios occurs!

COMMISSIONER BARBARA HERSHELL: Actually, by all accounts, heaven is supposed to be on the side of justice, so I am not sure that would be where to inquire for help.

PETER GOODMAN: Counselor Godwin, I am not sure about your examples. Couldn't I, equally, suppose that we decided in your favor, leading to an improved lot for chimpanzees and for the fullfledged Turing 346s (which we will now switch on only with a great deal of fatherly forethought). Couldn't we also suppose a third scenario in which the metalloids come down the ramp and shout, "Sniveling tokenism! Death to the mammalian slime: metalloids only!" And they proceed to exterminate us humans. In my fourth scenario, the chimpanzee-like chauvinists consume us all in a series of barbecues.

So I balance your science-fiction horror-tales with my science-fiction horror-tales. Why do you think there is something distinctive about yours?

MARY GODWIN: If there arc irrational chauvinist monsters out there, then there are irrational chauvinist monsters out there. With them, questions of justice and right cannot be debated.

But my tales—and you all recognized it too—appeal to a natural extension of our parochial morality, to a broad conception of personhood, one consistent with the extension to all humans that we have already made, albeit fitfully and incompletely. And I have employed the same imaginative tool that was used, historically, in forging this extension: to imagine that the now powerful are powerless and the now powerless are powerful, and to ask, given this, whether a rough sense of justice, common to both power distributions, comes to mind.

COMMISSIONER KLAUS VERSEN: Does it, Commissioners?

Notes and Suggestions for
  Further Reading

The First Morning
About human and chimpanzee genetics, see, for example, Jorge Yunis, Kelly Dunham, and Jeffrey Sawyer, "The Striking Resemblance of High-Resolution G-Banded Chromosomes of Man and Chimpanzee," *Science* 208 (6 June 1980), 1145–48. See also "Chinese May Resume Experiments to Create 'Near-Human' Ape," *Houston Post* (from *Chicago Tribune*), February 15, 1981, Section A, p. 19. A Dr. Ji Yongxiang, now head of a regional university, claimed that, in a 1967 experiment in Shenyang, a human male made pregnant a chimpanzee female. The experiment was terminated in the third month by cultural revolutionaries who sent the experimenters, including Yongxiang, off to farm labor. The chimpanzee apparently died of neglect. Dr. Yongxiang and his colleagues supposed that offspring might take on lonely and unpleasant tasks such as shepherding and deep mining, or provide "spare parts" for organ transplants to humans.

Mary Godwin (née Wollstonecraft), 1759–1797, wrote *A Vindication of the Rights of Women* in response to Edmund Burke's conservative *Reflections on the Civil War in France*. Strangely, she wrote it while residing in Thomas Taylor's house. She died shortly after giving birth to Mary Wollstonecraft Godwin (Shelley), 1797–1851. Mother and daughter both "ran off to the Continent" to live with lovers whom they latterly married. Both were scorned as scandalous atheistical hussies during their lifetimes. Peter Singer cites Taylor's *Vindication of the Rights of Brutes* in his *Animal Liberation* (New York: Avon, 1977). Taylor, incidentally, was known in his time as "The Platonist," not so much for producing the first complete translation of Plato's works into English (under the patronage of the Duke of Norfolk, the edition was printed and installed in the Duke's library, but not offered for public sale, perhaps because Plato was a pagan), but for proclassical writings

71

and translations, including the anti-Christian arguments of the Roman Emperor Julian. He was reputed to have statues of pagan gods in his study, to pour libations to them, and to have been expelled by his landlady for trying to sacrifice a bull in his room. The final accusation is likely to be false, for he was a happily married home-owner and hence unlikely to have had a landlady, much less a bull. (See L. S. Boas's introduction to Taylor's *Vindication of the Rights of Brutes* [Gainesville, Fla.: Scholars' Facsimiles & Reprints, 1966].)

Alan Turing's description of a universal computing device, subsequently called a "universal Turing machine," is "On Computable Numbers, with an Application to the *Entscheidungsproblem*," *Proceedings of the London Mathematical Society*, Series 2–42 (Nov. 17, 1936), pp. 230–265. His description of the "imitation game," appears in "Computing Machinery and Intelligence," *Mind*, Vol. 59, No. 236 (1950). That essay, along with related pieces, appears in *The Mind's I*, ed. Douglas Hofstadter and Daniel Dennett (New York: Basic Books, 1981). Something virtually identical to Turing's test appears in René Descartes's *Discourse on Method*:

If there were such machines having the organs and the shape of a monkey or of some other nonrational animal, we would have no way of telling whether or not they were of the same nature as these animals; if instead they resembled our bodies and imitated so many of our actions as far as this is morally possible, we would always have two very certain means of telling that they were not, for all that, true men. The first means is that they would never use words or other signs, putting them together as we do in order to tell our thoughts to others. For one can well conceive of a machine being so made as to pour forth words, and even words appropriate to the corporeal actions that cause a change in its organs—as, when one touches it in a certain place, it asks what one wants to say to it, or it cries out that it has been injured, and the like—but it could never arrange its words differently so as to answer to the sense of all that is said in its presence, which is something even the most backward men can do. The second means is that, although they perform many tasks very well or perhaps can do them better than any of us, they inevitably fail in other tasks; by this means one would discover that they do not act through knowledge, but only through the disposition of their organs. For while reason is a universal instrument that can be of help in all sorts of circum-

stances, these organs require a particular disposition for each particular action; consequently, it is morally impossible for there to be enough different devices in a machine to make it act in all of life's situations in the same way as our reason makes us act.*

The work of Turing and others on computability, and the practical development of increasingly powerful electronic computers, seemingly has forced us to think that Descartes was quite wrong in his confidence that no "mere machine" could pass the Descartes/Turing test.

Indira Ramajan's view about personhood is given current-day expression in Derik Parfit, *Reasons and Persons* (Oxford: The University Press, 1984); this book gives a penetrating examination of the notion of person, arguing that our age-old notion of person as unitary, indivisible substance evaporates in face of recent scientific and philosophical developments. Leibniz's views may be found in *Monadology* and *First Truths*; Spinoza's in *Rules for the Improvement of the Understanding* and *Ethics*.

The Afternoon

An account of Alan Turing's life, and a reasonable nontechnical account of his ideas, may be found in Andrew Hodges, *Alan Turing: The Enigma*, (New York: Simon & Schuster, 1983). He headed a World War II team which broke the German "Enigma" coding machine, in part by taking most major steps toward electronic computing. He had a hand in the building of the first electronic computers. Prosecuted for homosexuality, as an alternative to prison he was forced to take hormones that made him impotent. He died by eating an apple laced with potassium cyanide.

Joseph Weizenbaum, who wrote the ELIZA program, gives a clear account of Turing machines and of his own worries about computers in *Computer Power and Human Reason* (San Francisco: W. H. Freeman, 1976). His account, while passionate and clearly religious, remains ambiguous in that he seems to suggest that humans have a *choice*, which he hopes will be negative, about

---

* Donald A. Cress, tr., Descartes, *Discourse on Method* (Indianapolis: Hackett Publishing Co., 1980), p. 30.

whether computers will become persons. It is hard to tell whether Weizenbaum is claiming that computers *cannot* (ever and in principle) be persons, or that we shouldn't *allow them to become* persons. This ambiguity abets Weizenbaum's computer-phobia. If he straightforwardly argued that machines cannot be persons, then we should hardly be expected to worry much about computers. If he admitted that they could become persons but argued that we should not allow them to do so, then he produce a missing (and perhaps nakedly superstitious) argument to the effect that each and every "artificial" person *must be evil* and should therefore not be allowed. This is the genesis of the Hollywood version of Frankenstein's monster: A nonnatural, human-like creature *must* be evil.

The view that the human mind is itself a host of independent components, as AL might be thought of as a host of ELIZA programs, has dominated the last decade of cognitive psychology; see, for example, Jerry Fodor, *The Modularity of Mind* (Cambridge: MIT Press, 1983).

Isaac Newton, among others, wondered whether four colors would be sufficient to color a map so that no two adjoining countries would have the same color. See K. Appel and Wolfgang Haken, "The Solution to the Four-Color-Map Problem," *Scientific American,* Vol. 237, No. 4 (1977), pp. 108–120. The proof, being too long for a human mathematician to work through, was achieved by the computer. For some time the University of Illinois (Urbana-Champaign) canceled its postage with "Four Colors Suffice." Indira Ramajan is perhaps too cynical about Turing's conjecture that electronic computers would make humans with mathematical talent seem less impressive. In science fiction of the 1930s we find that the most revered spacemen, that is, the astrogators, are called "computers"; one finds in E. E. Smith's *Spacehounds of IPC* (New York: Ace, 1947), p. 6 (originally published by Radio-Science Publications in 1931), " 'Hi, Breck!,' the burly one called, as he strode up to the instrument-desk of the chief pilot and tossed his bag carelessly into a corner. 'Behold your computer in the flesh! What's all this howl and fuss about poor computation?' " For a theoretical proof that a universal Turing machine

computer can reproduce itself or create a machine of greater complexity, see John Von Neumann, "General and Logical Theory of Automata," in *Collected Works* Vol. 5, ed. A. H. Taub (New York: Macmillan, 1963), pp. 288–328, particularly pp. 312–318.

The basic results of Alan and Beatrice Gardner's work with the female chimpanzee, Washoe, first appeared in "Teaching Sign Language to a Young Chimpanzee," *Science* 165 (1969): 664–672. For an informal account of gorilla IQ testing, see Francine Patterson and Eugene Linden, *The Education of Koko* (New York: Holt, Rinehart & Winston, 1981). For a range of views about ape-signing, including some quite negative commentary, see Thomas Sebeok and Jean Umiker-Sebeok, eds., *Speaking of Apes* (New York: Plenum, 1980). For my views see Justin Leiber, "The Strange Creature," in R. Harre and V. Reynolds, eds., *The Meaning of Primate Signals* (Cambridge: The University Press, 1984), pp. 77–88 (a slightly different version appears, under the title "The vindication of the language organ," in *New Ideas in Psychology*, Vol. 1, No. 2, pp. 157–168). Most actual ape researchers seem to agree that apes "use signs" and "mean"; disagreements concern the degree to which apes can be said to produce sentences.

Curiously, very recent work has strongly confirmed Thomas Taylor's argument that we fail to recognize that monkeys speak to one another because their speech is too difficult or unfamiliar to us. For example, Dorothy L. Cheney and Robert M. Seyfarth (see their work in Harre and Reynolds above) have shown that vervet-monkey young are taught by their parents to produce vocal signals that warn, distinguishably, of danger-from-a-leopard, danger-from-a-snake, danger-from-an-eagle, and danger-strange-vervet. But, though vervets, and audiographical analysis, distinguish these cries, human beings cannot hear the difference.

The Second Morning

What I have called "the-cast-of-millions" argument appears in Ned Block, "Troubles With Functionalism," in C. Wade Savage, ed., *Minnesota Studies in the Philosophy of Science* Vol. 9: *Perception and Cognition* (Minneapolis: University of Minneapolis Press, 1978), pp. 261–325. The Chinese-Box argument, with peer com-

mentary, appears in J. Searle, "Minds, Brains, and Programs," *The Behavioral and Brain Sciences*, Vol. 3, No. 3 (1980), pp. 417–458. It also appears, with further commentary, in *The Mind's I* (see above). For a good collection of classical and recent philosophic views, see John Perry, ed., *Personal Identity* (Berkeley: University of California Press, 1975); see also his *Dialogue on Personal Identity and Immortality* (Indianapolis: Hackett Publishing Co., 1978). René Descartes's *Meditations* gives perhaps the most influential expression of the view that mind and body are wholly separate substances.

The view that solipsism, and the "absolute privacy" of personal experience, arises from "grammatical" features of our language has been made popular by Ludwig Wittgenstein (see, for example, his *Philosophical Investigations* (New York: Macmillan, 1953). It is not clear if Wittgenstein thought of this as limited to particular human languages, for he nowhere considers the human languages that significantly differ pronominally from English, German, and other European languages. In Old Japanese, for example, there were no personal pronouns, only expressions indicating "here" or "elsewhere"; some linguists maintain that even Modern Japanese lacks real personal pronouns, although it has a large number of nouns that convey such information. In *Beyond Rejection* (New York: Ballantine Books, 1980, excerpted in *The Mind's I*), I imagine my protagonist to wake up with a female body but remembering a male one, the result of a mind implant. I wrote in the first person to avoid the sexed pronouns, "he" and "she," of the English third person. I would not have had that option in Berber, which requires a specification of sex in first, second, and third person.

Sarah Blaffer Hrdy's, *The Langurs of Abu* (Cambridge: Harvard University Press, 1977), brilliantly shows us how monkey communities can substantially mirror our own individual and collective conflicts between males and females; see also her *The Woman that Never Evolved* (Cambridge: Harvard University Press, 1981).